The Teenage Boy's Playbook on Sex and Relationships:

From Rookie to MVP with 20 Simple Rules

S. De Lisle

Copyright © 2013 by S. De Lisle

All rights reserved.

ISBN: 1478348801

ISBN-13: 9781478348801

Trois Boys Press

**This book is dedicated to my MVPs:
Dustin, Aaron and Grayson**

Introduction

Sex and sports share some important similarities:

- You need to be mentally and physically prepared before you play.

- You must follow the rules or suffer the penalties.

- And best of all, if done right, you will receive years of enjoyment from both.

There is at least one major difference between them, though. With sports, your parents and coaches teach you the ins and outs of the game and show you how to improve your skills. Not so much with sex and relationships. Somehow young men are supposed to magically know how to behave around girls—and make good choices about sex. But these important life skills need to be taught, just like the proper techniques for swinging a bat or throwing a spiral.

This simple rulebook has everything you need to take the mystery out of your relationships with the opposite sex. Follow it, and when the time is right, you're sure to be an all-star.

Rule #1
Learning From Your Coaches

Your parents were your first coaches. And, although they may seem old and out-of-touch with your life right now, they know a thing or two about what it's like to be a teenager—and more importantly, they are your biggest fans. Hopefully, your parents will initiate a conversation with you about sex and relationships. But, if they don't, don't be afraid to ask *them*. That's what parents (and coaches) are for: to help you decide when it's best to pass, run or punt. For more tips on how to get the sex conversation going with your parents, see page 43.

S. DE LISLE

With Age, Comes Wisdom:

In 2011, the average age of an NFL head coach was fifty.

THE TEENAGE BOY'S PLAYBOOK ON SEX AND RELATIONSHIPS

Rule #2

Free Agency

It's OK *not* to have a girlfriend. Really, it is. You will have plenty of time later on to make a commitment to a girl. Right now, you're learning about *your* likes and dislikes. Sometimes, in a relationship, you worry so much about pleasing the other person it prevents you from getting to know yourself. For the time being, consider going out with girls in large groups. You'll learn a lot about the opposite sex by just hanging out with them and observing them. Think of it like watching tape; the information you gather now will be useful down the road.

Anything Good Is Worth Waiting for...

In the United States, the median age for men to marry is 28.3. For women, it's 25.8.

Rule #3

Going to Practice

You wouldn't play in the World Series without first swinging your bat a few times. "Going to the batting cages" can give you the confidence you need when it's time to "step up to the plate" for real. And it helps release some of the sexual tension that could cause you to "put your bat in the wrong dugout." Masturbation is a completely normal and healthy activity for boys *and* girls- no need to be embarrassed. However, since masturbation is not generally recognized as a spectator sport, make sure you "practice" in private.

Not everyone wants to masturbate, and that's OK, too. To each his own. Whether you masturbate or not, though, there's a good chance you will have a wet dream, which is when a boy or man ejaculates in his sleep. So, if you wake up with sticky sheets and a smile on your face, don't be alarmed.

And to Think It Might Be Good For You, Too!

According to a study in the Journal of the American Medical Association, men who masturbate frequently have a lower incidence of prostate cancer.

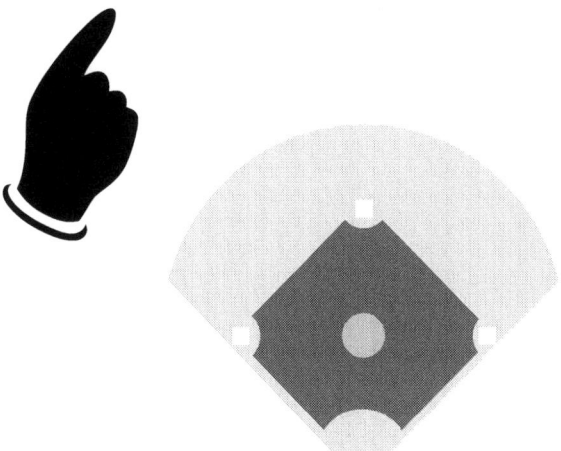

Rule #4

Eligibility

There's a reason all professional sports teams have minimum ages players must reach before they can join the team: They want to make sure players are mature enough to handle the responsibility and pressure that come with being a world class athlete. The NFL is the strictest, insisting that players be at least three years removed from high school before they are eligible to play. The NBA is more lenient, requiring that players be out of high school for a minimum of one year. And the NHL and MLB require that their players be at least 18 years of age. Since there are minimum age requirements for playing professional sports, it's only fitting that there should be a minimum age requirement for having sex. After all, sex can result in you becoming a father, which is way more responsibility and pressure than playing on any professional sports team.

Although three years out of high school may not be a realistic wait for some young men, you should at least consider waiting until you have graduated from high school and are out of your parents' house. Not only will your parents appreciate that simple courtesy, you won't have to sneak around in fear of your parents catching you "sliding into home."

Truth and Consequences

According to a 2010 study by the Yale University School for Public Health, teenage parents are less educated and have a significantly lower lifetime earning potential.

Rule #5

Know Where Your Receiver Is At All Times

A quarterback and receiver must completely trust each other and know exactly what the other is doing in order to complete a pass. Similarly, you must make sure you are on the same page with your girlfriend about the "route you will be running"—or how much each of you is comfortable committing to the other, emotionally and sexually. Sex is not just a physical act; it's an emotional one too. Having casual sex can lead to hurt feelings, because exposing yourself—physically and emotionally—to another person can make you feel vulnerable. You may be surprised by how a girl—who seemed completely independent with her clothes on—can turn into an obsessed, demanding "uberfan" once she's taken her clothes off. Conversely, you may be surprised by your own emotions as well! Be patient and understanding if you and your partner are not on the same page when it comes to sex. And even if you agree about things right now, allow each other to change your minds without penalty. If the two of you don't communicate well, your relationship will have a zero percentage of completion.

Worse yet, you may hurt someone you care about.

Save the Hurt for the Football Field

After surveying hundreds of sexually active teenagers, researchers found that girls were more than twice as likely as boys to say they "felt bad about themselves" after having sex. Girls were also more than three times as likely to say they felt used as a result of having sex.

Rule #6

The Referee Calls the Shots

In any sexual encounter, the girl is the referee. You are the big, strong guy, so the presumption is that you could overpower any girl and force her to have sexual relations with you. Of course most young men would never think about doing something so terrible. However, if at **ANY** point, she tells you "no" or "stop"—even after the two of you have agreed to have sex or have had sex previously—you **MUST** obey her request! If you don't, the "technical foul" you receive will involve prison time.

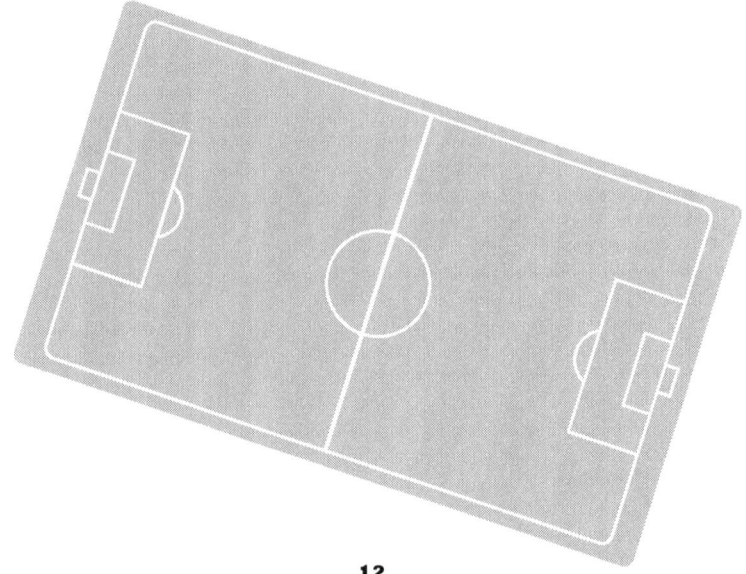

A Loser's Game Plan

In one study, more than 30% of male college students surveyed admitted to using force or emotional pressure to obtain sex from a girl.

Rule #7

Proper Equipment

You would be insane not to wear protective equipment when you play tackle football. The same is true when you have sex: A proper fitting condom is a must. Even if your girlfriend says she's on birth control pills, you still need to wear a condom! After all, the pill can't protect either of you from sexually transmitted diseases (STDs). So, unless you are prepared to risk getting infected with an STD (or becoming a father), you should **always** wear protection. There's no reason not to wear a condom. If you are embarrassed to buy or wear condoms, you probably aren't ready to be having sex. There's nothing wrong with waiting on the bench until you are sure it's time to "get in the game."

Player Errors

As good as condoms are, they are not foolproof. The Center for Disease Control and Prevention estimates that condoms are effective 82%-98% of the time. The majority of condom failure is a result of improper usage, including using condoms that are poorly fitting, condoms that are expired, or previously used condoms (Foul!) Make sure to read the instructions on the condom box before using one for the first time.

Rule #8

No Performance Enhancing Drugs

Using steroids and other performance enhancing drugs can get you kicked off most sports teams. However, drinking alcohol or using any mind altering drugs before engaging in sexual relations can result in even more serious consequences than that. If you are the one drinking or using drugs—which you shouldn't be if you are an athlete who respects his body—you cannot possibly make good decisions when you are chemically impaired. And, if the girl is high or drunk, **YOU** will be the one to blame if she decides she really didn't want to fool around with you after all. In the eyes of the law, she cannot consent to sex if she is intoxicated.

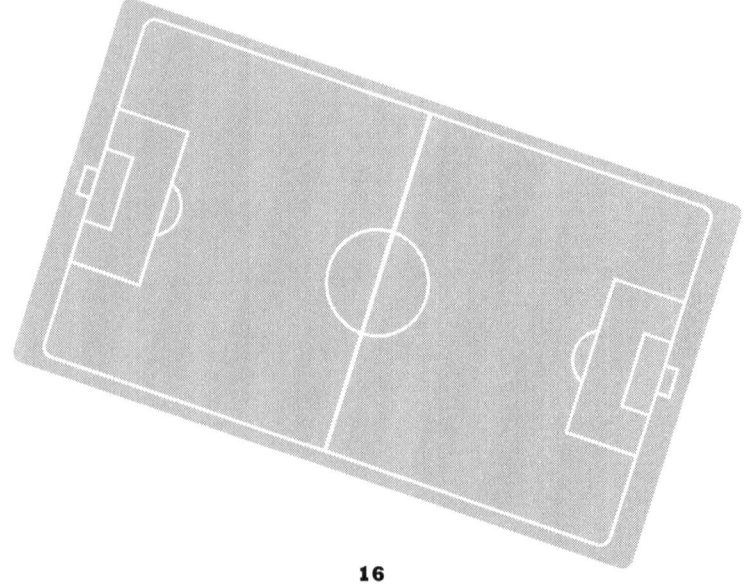

Get Your Head in the Game

According to the National Institutes of Health, in approximately half of all sexual assault cases, the victim, perpetrator or both were consuming alcohol prior to the assault.

Rule #9

Unsportsmanlike Conduct

A girl may tell you she wants to have sex with you—even if she's not really emotionally or physically ready for it—because she thinks that's what you want to hear. However, if you don't love or respect a girl, don't have sexual relations with her. Just **DON'T** do it. Not only is that selfish of you, but your one night of pleasure may end up coming back to haunt you later on. You see, a girl who is willing to offer up her body to you as some sort of a sacrifice is typically immature and insecure. These needy (and possibly unstable) girls are easy to recognize since they are often hypersexual and promiscuous, forcing themselves on you to the point where you may feel uncomfortable. As crazy as it sounds, this type of girl may even try to get pregnant with your baby as a way to get you to commit to her. If you come across a girl like this, put on your running shoes and sprint the other direction, before it's too late. Think of it this way: You know how your coaches have always told you that winning isn't everything; it's how you play the game that's most important? Well, having an orgasm, isn't everything either. How you conduct yourself in a relationship is what's most important. Better to implement Rule #3 than have sex with a girl you don't care about. And, by the way, when you do find a special someone who is mentally and physically prepared for sexual intimacy with you, make sure you consider her needs and desires. Being attentive to your partner is a sign of a good team player.

The Best of the Worst

Over the years, there have been some unforgettable—and unforgivable—moments in sports. Here are some of the lowlights of unsportsmanlike conduct:
- Kermit Washington Punches Rudy Tomjanovich, nearly killing him *Lakers vs. Rockets, December 9, 1977*
- Mike Tyson Bites Evander Holyfield's Ear *June 28, 1997*
- Elizabeth Lambert Yanks Opponent to Ground by Ponytail in College Soccer Game
  New Mexico vs. Brigham Young, November 5, 2009

Rule #10

Minor Leagues

Of course there are other ways to be sexually intimate with someone besides sexual intercourse, including kissing, petting (touching a girl's breasts or each other's genitals), oral sex, and "outercourse" (rubbing your genitals against your partner's). Just remember it is still possible to contract STDs from most of these alternatives to intercourse. Wherever there's bodily fluid and/or mucous membranes, there will be the bacteria and viruses that cause STDs. And, like intercourse, all these warm-ups leading to "the big show" have an emotional and mental component, too. After all, the mind and body are intimately connected. (Any baseball player who's in a mental hitting slump can verify the accuracy of the mind-body connection for you.)

There's a Reason They're Called Minor

Most MLB players spend at least some time in the minor leagues before being brought up to the majors. Compared to the salaries players make in the Big League, it's no surprise why the minor leagues are called "minor." Check out the average monthly salary of the three tiers of MLB's farm teams:
Triple A - $2150
Double A - $1500
Single A - $850-$1050

Rule #11

Unnecessary Roughness

Even in competitive sports there are penalties for being too rough. And, although there are many similarities between sex and sports, there is **NO** room for force or violence in the bedroom. Period.

That Hurts

20% of teens who have been in a serious relationship report being hit, slapped or pushed by a partner.

Rule #12

Team Bonding

You spend a lot of time with your teammates and some of them may be your best friends. However, locker rooms are notoriously overflowing with testosterone, and thus are not necessarily the best place to learn the nuances about girls and sex. Don't be influenced by teammates or friends who brag about their sexual conquests, which may or may not be real. When it comes to getting advice about girls, seek the input of older boys, siblings or parents who understand that intimacy has more to do with personal bests than breaking records. And don't you be that guy in the locker room (or elsewhere), bragging about your sexual encounters with your girlfriend. Your relationship with her is supposed to be based on trust. If it isn't, you shouldn't be having sexual relations with her anyway.

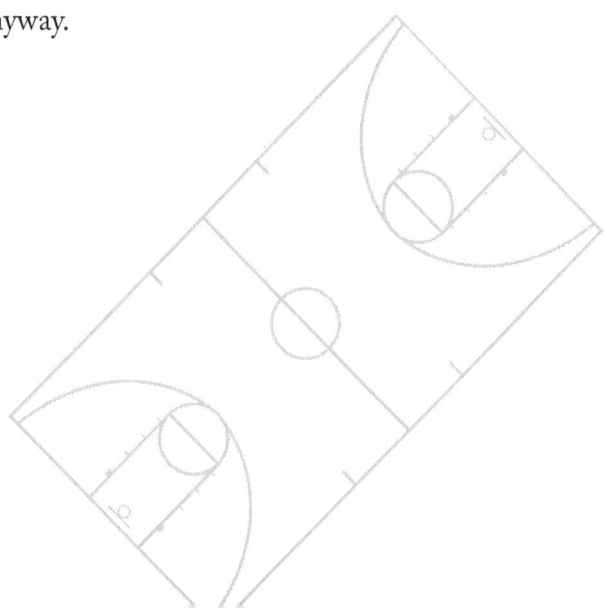

The King of Kissing and Telling

NBA superstar Wilt Chamberlain wrote a biography about his sexual exploits in which he claimed to have slept with more than 20,000 women. If true, that would mean he had sex with approximately 416 women every year. Before his death, he had regrets about his excessive promiscuity, "With all of you men out there who think that having a thousand different ladies is pretty cool, I have learned in my life I've found out that having one woman a thousand different times is much more satisfying."

Rule #13

Switching Teams

At some point, you may decide to "switch teams." Maybe you and your girlfriend aren't as compatible as you thought. Or maybe you just want to be on your own for a while. Sometimes being in a relationship causes you to feel like you are losing your own identity, and you may find that you need a break from being someone's boyfriend to find yourself again. Whatever the reason for breaking up with a girl, make sure you tell her right away. Don't drag things out when you know the relationship isn't going anywhere. And break up with her gently. No one wants to be dumped via text message. Since you have been in a relationship with this girl, you owe it to her to tell her face-to-face, in a kind, direct way. Otherwise you'll risk being despised by your ex and all her friends.

Hero or Traitor?

Fans love their players. Which is why when a player decides to leave, some fans take it very personally. Just consider how hometown fans reacted when the following players moved on to play for rival teams:
- LeBron James (Cavaliers to Heat)
- Brett Favre (Packers to "Retirement" to Jets to Vikings)
- Wade Boggs and Johnny Damon (Red Sox to Yankees)
- Shaquille O'Neal (Magic to Lakers)
- Chris Chelios (Blackhawks to Red Wings)

Rule #14

Getting Traded

There is a chance, as awful as it sounds, that your girlfriend may decide to "trade" you. Her breaking up with you might come as a complete shock, or you might have seen the writing on the wall and ignored it. You may not agree with her reason for leaving—maybe she won't even give you a reason. Whatever the case may be, don't beg her to reconsider. Or worse, get angry with her. A relationship requires *two* committed people. If she doesn't want to be in a relationship anymore, that's her prerogative, and you need to honor that. Besides, when a player gets traded, you don't want to see him whining about it. Walking off the field graciously will get you picked up by another "team" much quicker, and in the long run you will feel better about preserving your dignity.

Trading Up

Sometimes a trade works out for the better. Just ask the sports teams that benefitted from these fortuitous trades:
- Boston Red Sox (Babe Ruth)
- Denver Broncos (John Elway)
- Philadelphia 76ers (Dr. J)
- Montreal Expos (Pedro Martinez)
- Chicago Bulls (Scottie Pippen)

Rule #15

Instant Replay

Some professional sports allow officials to review plays, so they can see what really happened in order to make a fair call. And, when you are in a relationship that ends, it's a good idea to replay what happened and learn from any mistakes that either "team" made. In the case of "reviewing plays" in a relationship, the assessment may not be instant. Sometimes we need to put some distance between ourselves and the relationship before we can figure out why it didn't work. Don't be surprised if you feel upset when a relationship ends, even if *you* are the one who ended it. When you spend a lot of time with a girl, and then suddenly she's gone, you are bound to miss her. Missing someone doesn't necessarily mean you should get back together, though. Sometimes the relationship just becomes like a bad habit. Take a time-out to process what you have learned, and if the relationship wasn't a healthy one, move on to be a better "teammate" somewhere else. You will most likely be in many relationships before you choose to settle down with one person. Or you may be someone who prefers to go solo for his whole career. Either way, instant (or even delayed) replay of your relationships is a good idea for your personal growth.

Soccer: The Final Frontier

MLB allows it to review the validity of home runs. The NBA relies on it to judge the timeliness of buzzer beater shots. The NHL checks tape to see whether the puck crossed the goal line or not. Even tennis players may challenge a referee's call and request an instant replay. Soccer may be the last widely watched professional sport that does not utilize video replay during the course of the game. The largest professional soccer leagues, MLS and FIFA (the Fédération Internationale de Football Association), believe the technology would take away the "human element" and be disruptive to the flow of the game—the same arguments the NFL used prior to adopting in-game instant replay. Interestingly, the MLS only allows for review of tape *after* a game, to examine red card suspension calls—far too late to reinstate a player who could have changed the outcome of the game.

Rule #16

Escaping the Double-Team

Some guys make their own rules when it comes to relationships, and will try to "play on more than one team" at the same time. That mentality doesn't work in the big leagues, and it won't work in real life either. You cannot commit to two girls at once. In baseball, it might be thrilling getting caught between two bases, having to dodge a fielder's tag before getting back to the safety of the bag. But in a relationship, things are different. Eventually you will always be called out. If you are dating one girl and find yourself tempted by a new girl, "tag up," or end it, with your girlfriend before getting involved with a new one. Two-timing is not only cruel and sleazy; it's a no-win situation, because you *will* get caught. If you find that you make a bad choice and end up hurting someone, the best thing to do is to own up and apologize. And next time, save the risky base running for the ball field.

Double Trouble?

In the NBA, putting two defensive players on a superstar like LeBron James or Michael Jordan can be an effective tactic for shutting down the offense. Unless, of course, your team happens to have sniper-like jump shot shooters like John Paxson and Steve Kerr of the 6-time NBA Champion Chicago Bulls. Whenever Jordan was being double teamed, he could count on these two to keep the offense on target.

Rule #17

Avoiding the Disabled List

Nothing will sideline you quicker in the game of love than getting an STD or getting your partner pregnant before you're ready to be a parent. These are lifelong consequences that could force you into an "early retirement." After all, some sexually transmitted diseases are not curable and can even shorten your lifespan, like syphilis and AIDS. And, of course, once you get a girl pregnant, you are responsible for helping to raise that baby for the rest of your life. Always wear condoms and don't have sex until you are ready to accept any possible outcome of your sexual encounter. Some rules are worth repeating.

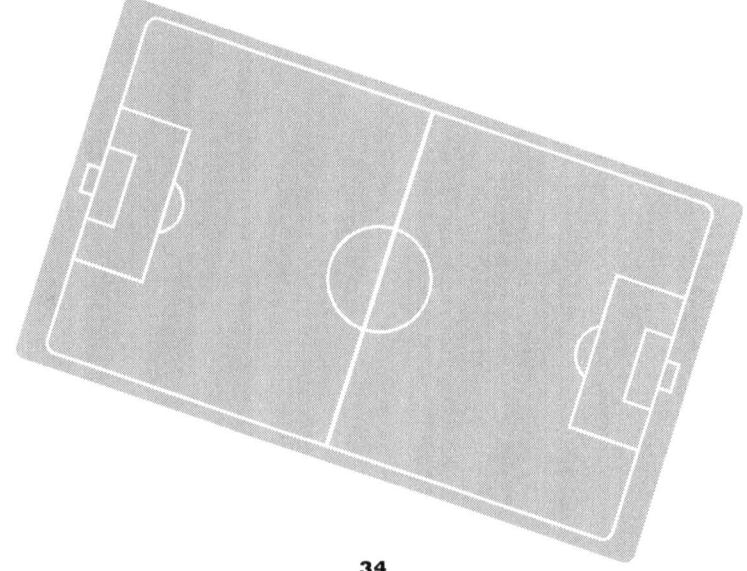

Disability Awareness

All professional sports leagues have their own disabled or injured reserve lists. This prevents a team from exceeding the league's maximum number of rostered players. In all but the NFL, a player on the disabled or injured reserve list may return to play in the same season in which he is placed on the disabled list. The MLB has two separate disabled lists: 15-day and 60-day. A baseball player may not return to active status before the appropriate time has elapsed, with the countdown to eligibility beginning on the day of the first missed game.

Rule #18

Playing Man-to-Man

It's the 21st Century, so it's time to acknowledge that a large number of men (and women) are gay. Yes, even some professional sports players. Being a strong heterosexual male doesn't mean you have to put down gay people. And even more than that, it would be cool if you were secure enough to set the homophobes straight if they start insulting gays in front of you. Don't worry; the heterosexual girls will still be able to detect your manliness even if you defend gay people. In fact, a lot of girls will find you *more* attractive for being so comfortable with your own sexuality that you can stand up for others who are different than you. Most women love the strong, powerful, sensitive type. Be one.

No Penalties for Being Gay

Pro hockey player Sean Avery has twice led the NHL in penalty minutes, yet this "tough guy" had this to say about gay marriage: "Committed couples should be able to marry the person they love...I treat everyone the way I expect to be treated, and that applies to marriage."

Rule #19

Possession

Being in possession of the ball is critical for winning most sports. In relationships, possession of your ***integrity*** is the key. Do not change who you are to get someone to like you. If they don't like you the way you are, find someone who does. And you should never try to make a girl change for you either. There was a reason you were attracted to her in the first place; don't try to mold her to be someone she is not. Allow her to be herself and go out with her girlfriends. Two independent people make for a fulfilling and interesting relationship. Possess the ball, not the girl.

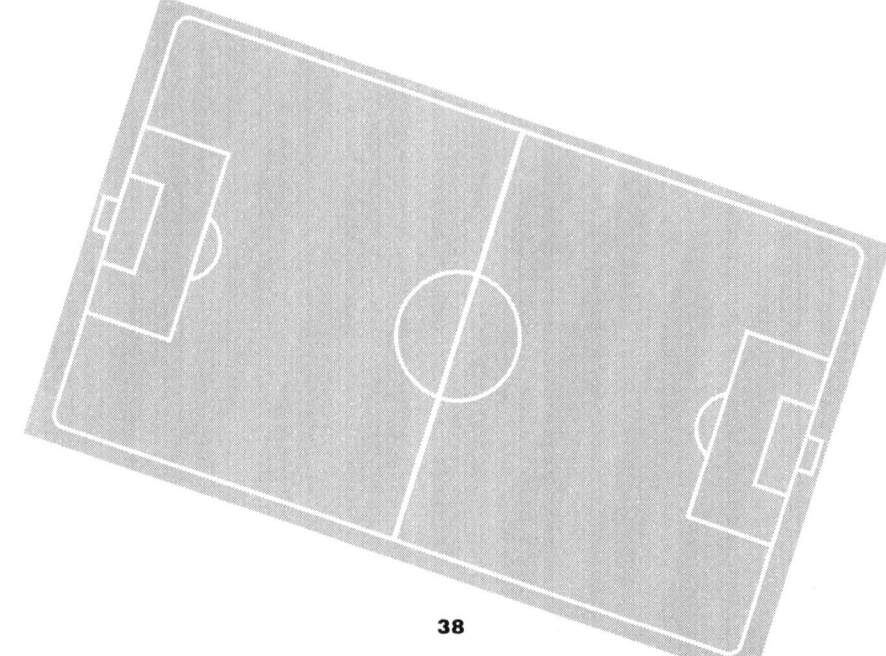

Got Balls?

In sports, especially football, it is widely accepted that the team that possesses the ball more, will win the game. The NFL even tracks this percentage for every team. However, in one interesting game on September 21, 2009 between the Miami Dolphins and the Indianapolis Colts, that assumption got turned on its head. The Colts won the game 27-23 even though they only had possession of the ball a mere 14:53—the lowest time of possession for a winning team in the NFL since 1977. The Colts ran 35 plays to the Dolphins 84. Sometimes it doesn't matter how many balls you possess; it's how you use them that matters most.

Rule #20

For the Love of the Game

Being sexually intimate with someone you love and trust is a natural and fulfilling part of every person's life. But, like alcohol, it is meant to be enjoyed by mature participants who are fully prepared to accept any of the possible consequences, like pregnancy and STDs. With that said, have fun with your sexuality, stay true to yourself, be kind to your partner—and wear a condom!

"In my contract I have the 'love of the game clause' that means I can play [basketball] anytime I want, any place I want."

Michael Jordan

HOW TO GET YOUR PARENTS OFF THE SIDELINES AND TALK TO YOU ABOUT SEX!

As I said at the beginning of this playbook, your parents are your first coaches and your biggest fans. Keep in mind, though, that your parents' coaches may not have instructed your parents about sex and relationships; and therefore, your parents may not know how to approach YOU to discuss these things. Another reason your parents may not have initiated "the talk" is because they may not be ready to accept that their "baby" is ready to discuss such sensitive topics. Sometimes we have a hard time believing our kids are growing up.

As a result, you may have to take the ball into your own hands. Ideally, it would be nice to get both parents' perspective, but if you are more comfortable talking with one parent over the other, start with the parent who you think will be more receptive. Below is a list of things you can say and/or do to get the conversation rolling:

1. Use this book! If a parent bought you this book, he or she is probably open to talking with you about sex. Pick a rule that you have a question about and bring the book to your parent. I have no problem if you

blame me, the author, for not being thorough enough in my explanations. Say something like: "Whoever wrote this book is very clever, but didn't explain [insert rule of your choice] very well; can you?"

2. Use this book—again! If you are reading this book without your parents' knowledge, put it down immediately! Just Kidding! Hand your parent(s) the book (or leave it in the bathroom where they're sure to read it) and tell them you would like their opinion on Rule #4 (or whatever rule appeals to you). Then follow up with them later to get their thoughts.

3. Use humor to lighten the mood. There's nothing like a joke to make it easier to broach a difficult topic. Try some of these one (or two) liners to initiate the sex talk:
   - "The last time the Tooth Fairy visited, she said the Stork would be coming to tell me about the "birds and the bees." Any idea when he's arriving?"
   - "You are far too young —and attractive — to be a grandparent, perhaps we should talk…"
   - "That 'Teen Mom' TV show sounds cool."
   - "Who wants to prevent STDs? **S**coring a **T**ouch **D**own is a good thing!"
   - "Was the Disney movie "The Odd Life of Timothy Green" based on a true story?"
   - "I only want to talk about sex because some day—in like thirty years, when I'm married and established in my career—I want to give you a grandchild."
   - "I just have one question about sex: who-what-where-when-why-how?"

- "When people say to use protection during sex, is that because in horror movies the teenagers always get attacked when they're making out?"
- "We're studying health in science, and I know this is very personal, but I am supposed to ask you about your oral habits." After your parent picks his or her jaw up off the floor, say, "I meant *hygiene*, but as long as we're on the other topic...."
- "Can you please explain the lyrics of [any sexually explicit Top 40 song] to me?" Note: Lady GaGa's "Disco Stick" or Katy Perry's "Peacock" would be great choices.

4. Blame your friend. "I have a friend who is thinking about having sex with his girlfriend, and I don't know what to tell him. Any ideas?" Normally, we shouldn't use our friends as scapegoats, but in this case, if it empowers you to get the conversation started, I say go for it. Just make sure not to name a real friend, otherwise your concerned parent might call your friend's parents. Now that's a conversation you don't want to have.

Regardless of what approach you take to initiate "the talk," make sure that your parent actually has the time in that moment to talk—your mom should not be leaving for work, or your dad should not be trying to get your little brother ready for school. Try having the conversation when you're alone with your parent—with perhaps a ball or gear shift between you. Talking with a parent about sex when you are shooting hoops, playing catch or driving in the car can make it less awkward.

Good luck, and remember: Your parents are your biggest fans, so no topic should be out-of-bounds.

References

All Internet sources are based on the content available at the given address between July 17 and July 19, 2012. If this content has changed or is no longer available, previous versions may be available through the Internet Archive at http://www.archive.org/index.php

Rule #1

Learning from Your Coaches

I averaged all the individual ages of the 2011 NFL head coaches listed on the NFL's website and came up with 50. http://www.nfl.com

Rule #2

Free Agency

The National Survey of Family Growth can be found here: www.cdc.gov/nchs/nsfg.htm

Rule #3
Going to Practice

Evidence linking masturbation to lowered risk of prostate cancer: Journal of American Medical Association masturbation study: Leitzmann MF, Platz EA, Stampfer MJ, Willett WC, Giovannucci E. (2004) *JAMA 291*. Ejaculation frequency and subsequent risk of prostate cancer, 1578-1586.

Rule #4

Eligibility

Yale study on teenage fathers:
http://news.yale.edu/2010/01/14/teenage-fathers-often-born-teenage-fathers-study-finds

Rule #5

Know Where Your Receiver Is At All Times

Survey of sexually active teens: Brady, S. (2007, Feb.) Adolescents' reported consequences of having oral sex versus vaginal sex. *Pediatrics*, (Vol. 119), 229-236.

Rule #6

The Referee Calls the Shots

Survey on campus sex: http://www.joyfulheartfoundation.org/campussafety_harmreductiontips.htm

Rule #7
Proper Equipment:

Condom statistics:
http://www.cdc.gov/reproductivehealth/unintendedpregnancy/contraception.htm

Rule #8

No Performance Enhancing Drugs

Statistics on sexual assault and alcohol usage: http://pubs.niaaa.nih.gov/publications/arh25-1/43-51.htm

Rule #9

Unsportsmanlike Conduct

2009 Top 13 Worst Examples of Unsportsmanlike Conduct: http://www.thetop13.com/worst-acts-of-unsportsmanlike-conduct-L23/

Rule #10

Minor Leagues

Information on minor league baseball: http://www.kidzworld.com/article/8352-minor-league-baseball

Rule #11

Unnecessary Roughness

Results of a 2006 Teen Abuse Study: http://www.caepv.org/getinfo/facts_stats.php?factsec=11

Rule #12

Team Bonding

One of Wilt Chamberlain's last interviews:
http://static.espn.go.com/nba/news/1999/1012/110905.html

Rule #13

Switching Teams

Some of the hardest player moves for fans to stomach: http://bleacherreport.com/articles/928925-derek-fisher-and-the-20-biggest-traitors-in-sports#/articles/928925-derek-fisher-and-the-20-biggest-traitors-in-sports/page/20

Rule #14

Getting Traded

List of lopsided player trades: http://espn.go.com/page2/s/readers/worstdeals.html

Rule #15

Instant Replay

Information and commentary on instant replay in professional soccer:
http://www.wired.com/business/2009/11/soccer-resists-the-instant-replay-despite-criticism/
http://blogs.providencejournal.com/ri-talks/this-new-england/2012/06/kent-jones-time-for-instant-replay-in-soccer.html

Rule #16

Escaping the Double-Team

Great resource for all things basketball: Frazier, W. & Sachare A. (1998). The idiot's guide to basketball. New York, NY: Penguin Books.

Rule #17
Avoiding the Disabled List:

Information on disability and injured reserves: http://www.wisegeek.com/in-baseball-what-is-a-disabled-list.htm

Rule #18

Playing Man-to-Man:

Article about Sean Avery's advocacy for gay marriage: http://www.nytimes.com/2011/05/08/sports/hockey/08avery.html

Rule #19

Possession

Analysis of unexpected 2009 Miami Dolphins and Indianapolis Colts game: http://scores.espn.go.com/nfl/recap?gameId=290921015

Rule #20:

For the Love of the Game:

Transcript of Michael Jordan's speech for his induction into the NBA Hall of Fame: http://www.sweetspeeches.com/s/1281-michael-jordan-michael-jordan-s-hall-of-fame-speech#ixzz20zKXQRLb

To order a copy of
The Teenage Boy's Playbook
on Sex and Relationships:
From Rookie to MVP with 20 Simple
Rules, please visit
www.teenageplaybook.com.

Made in the USA
Charleston, SC
26 December 2012